ICE CREAM SUNDAE COLORING BOOK

CRYSTAL
COLORING BOOKS

ISBN: 9781090496201

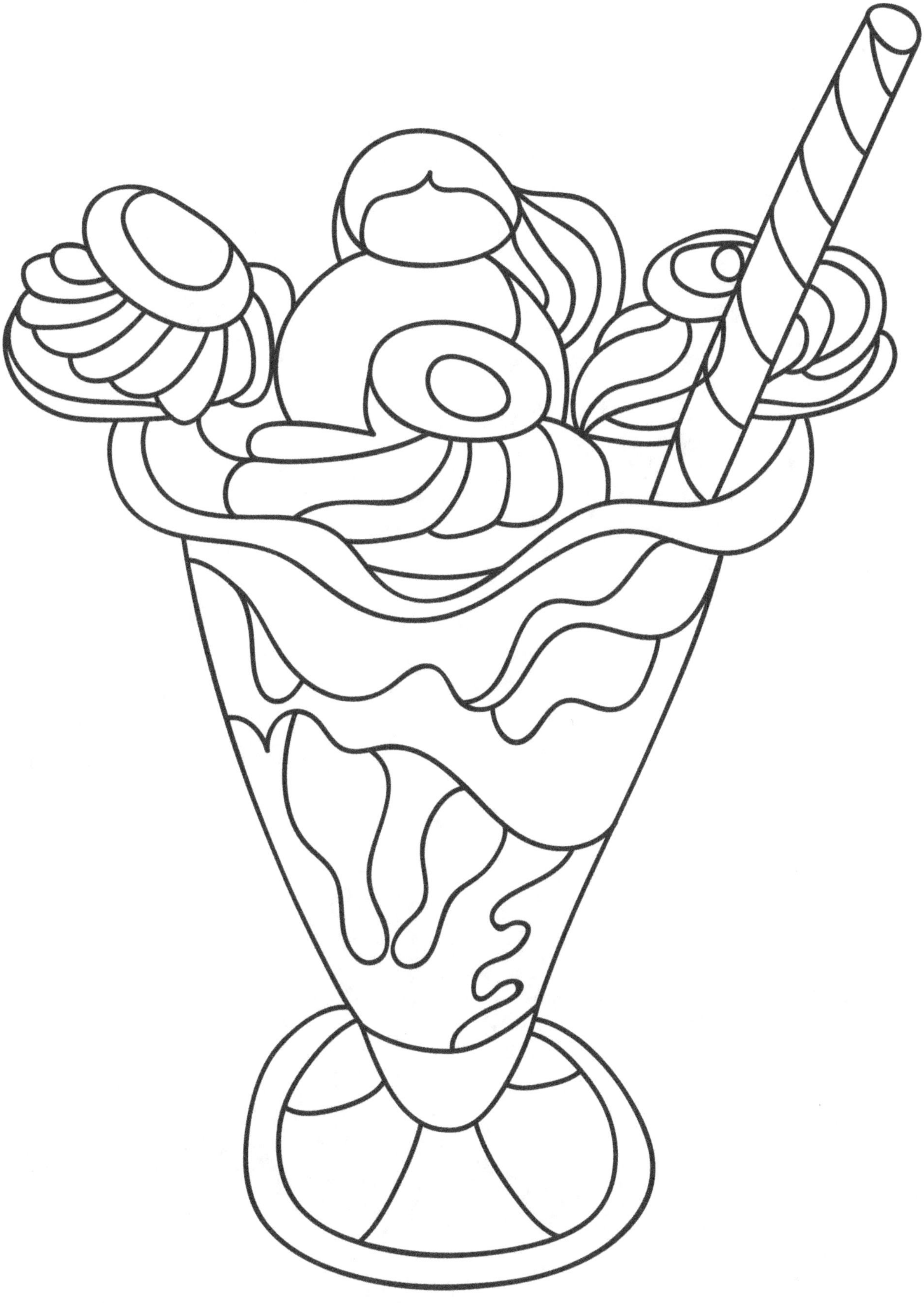

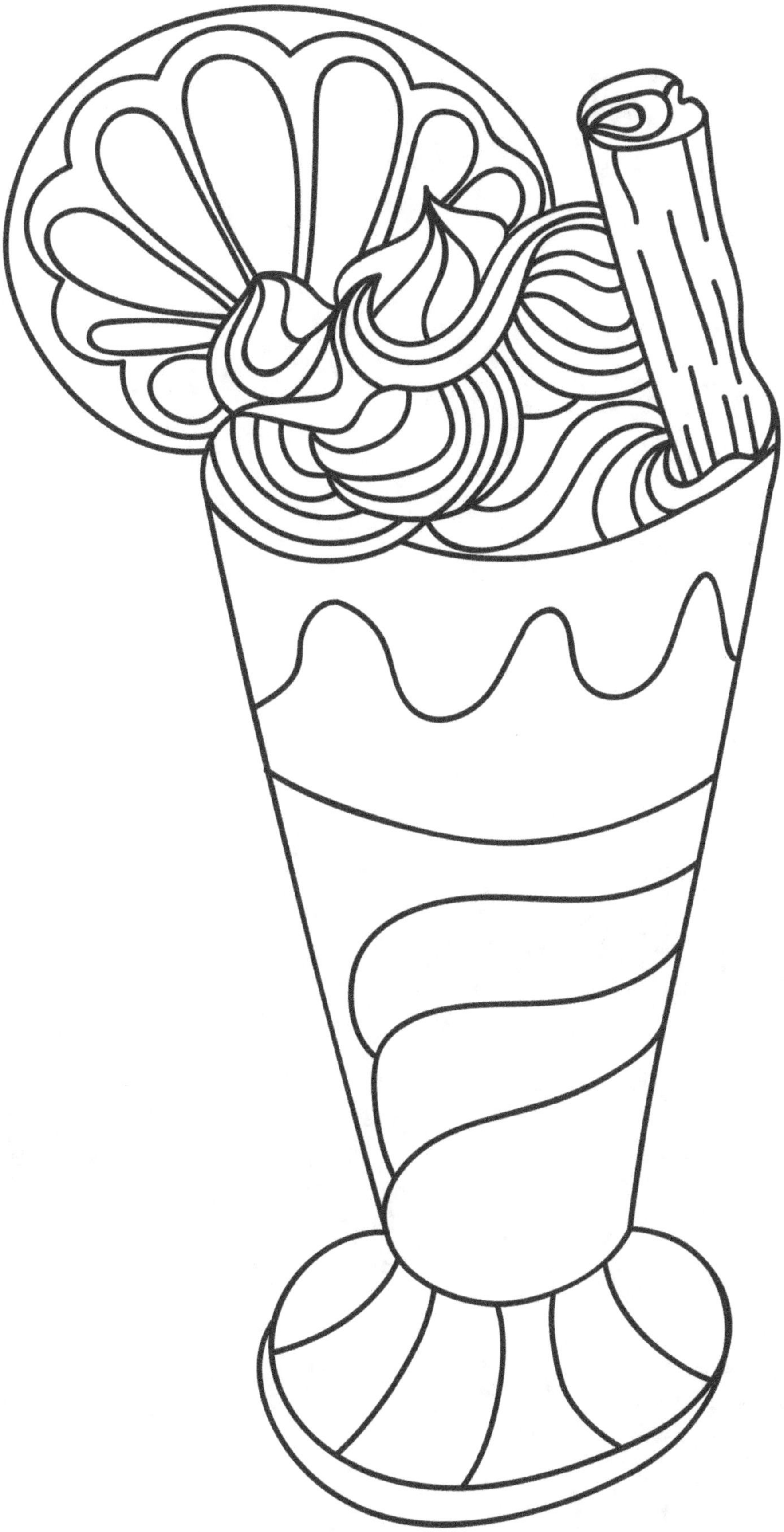

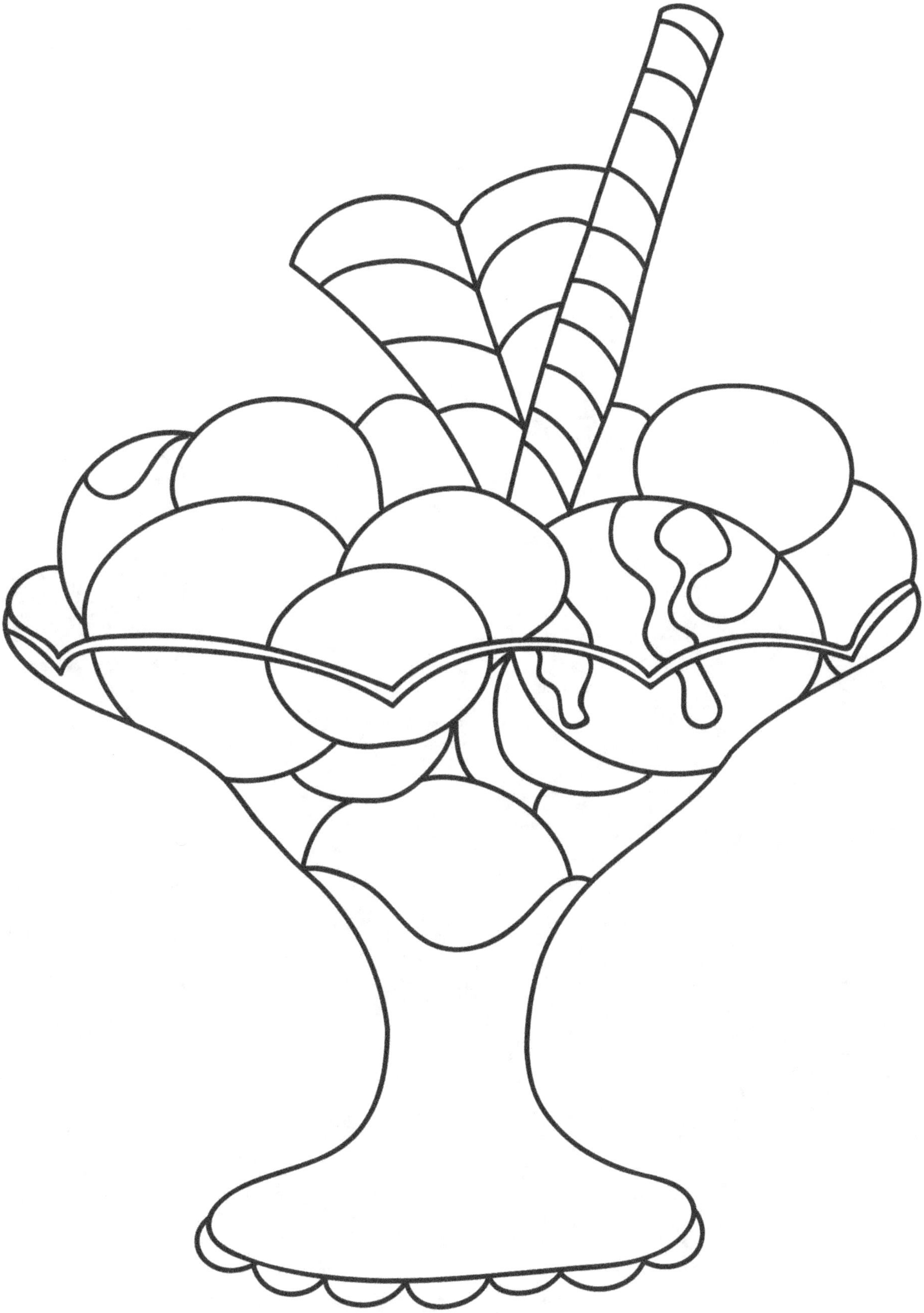

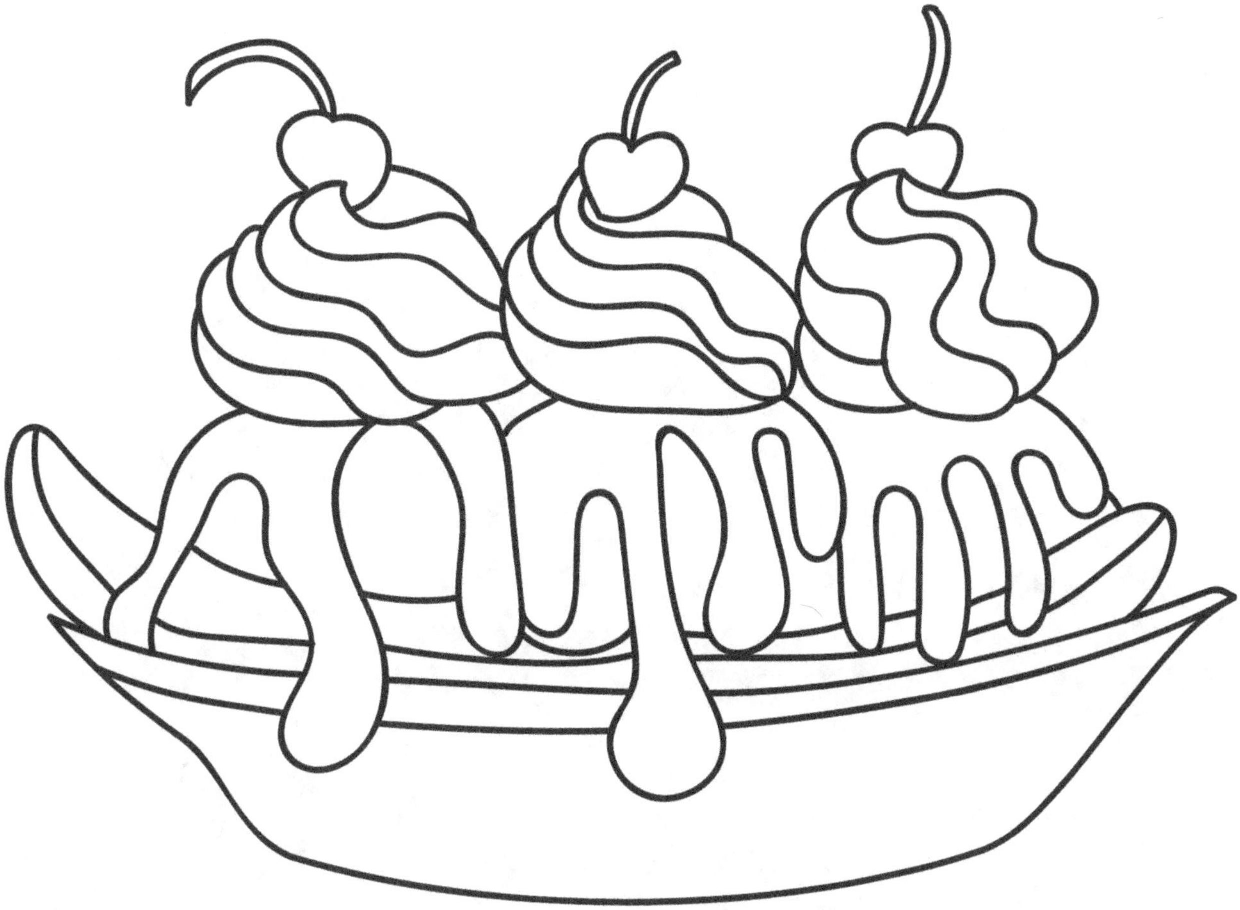

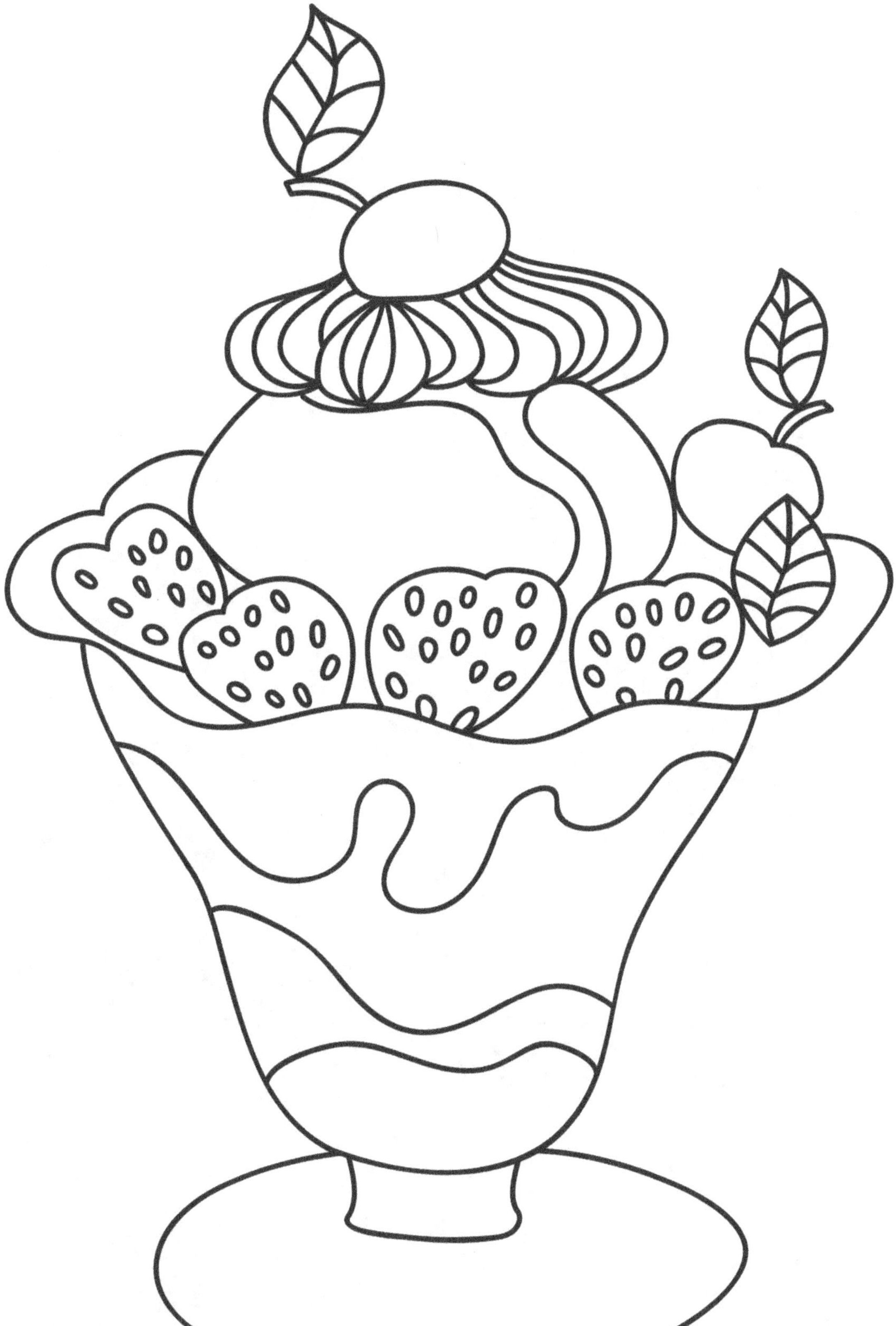

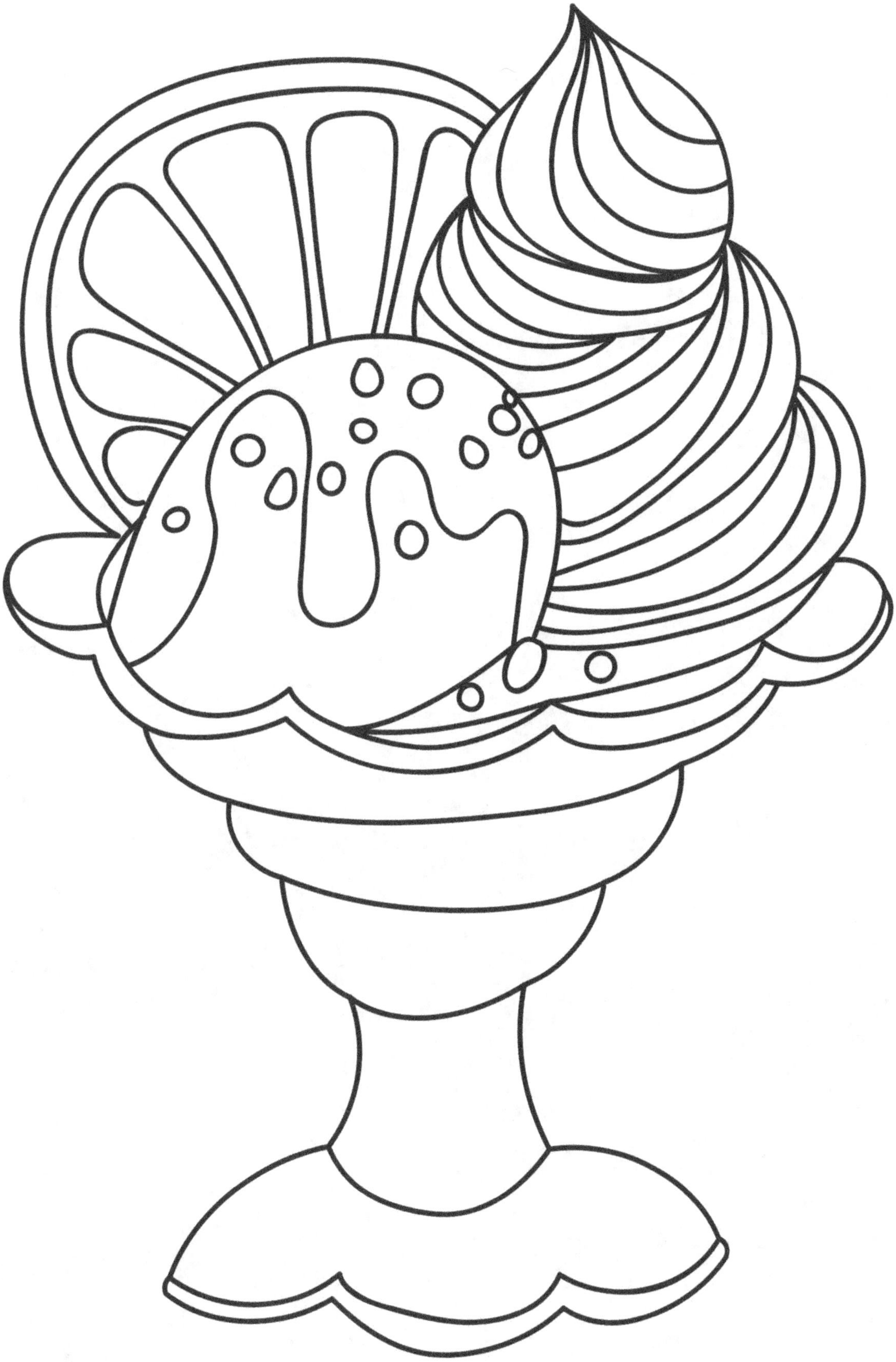

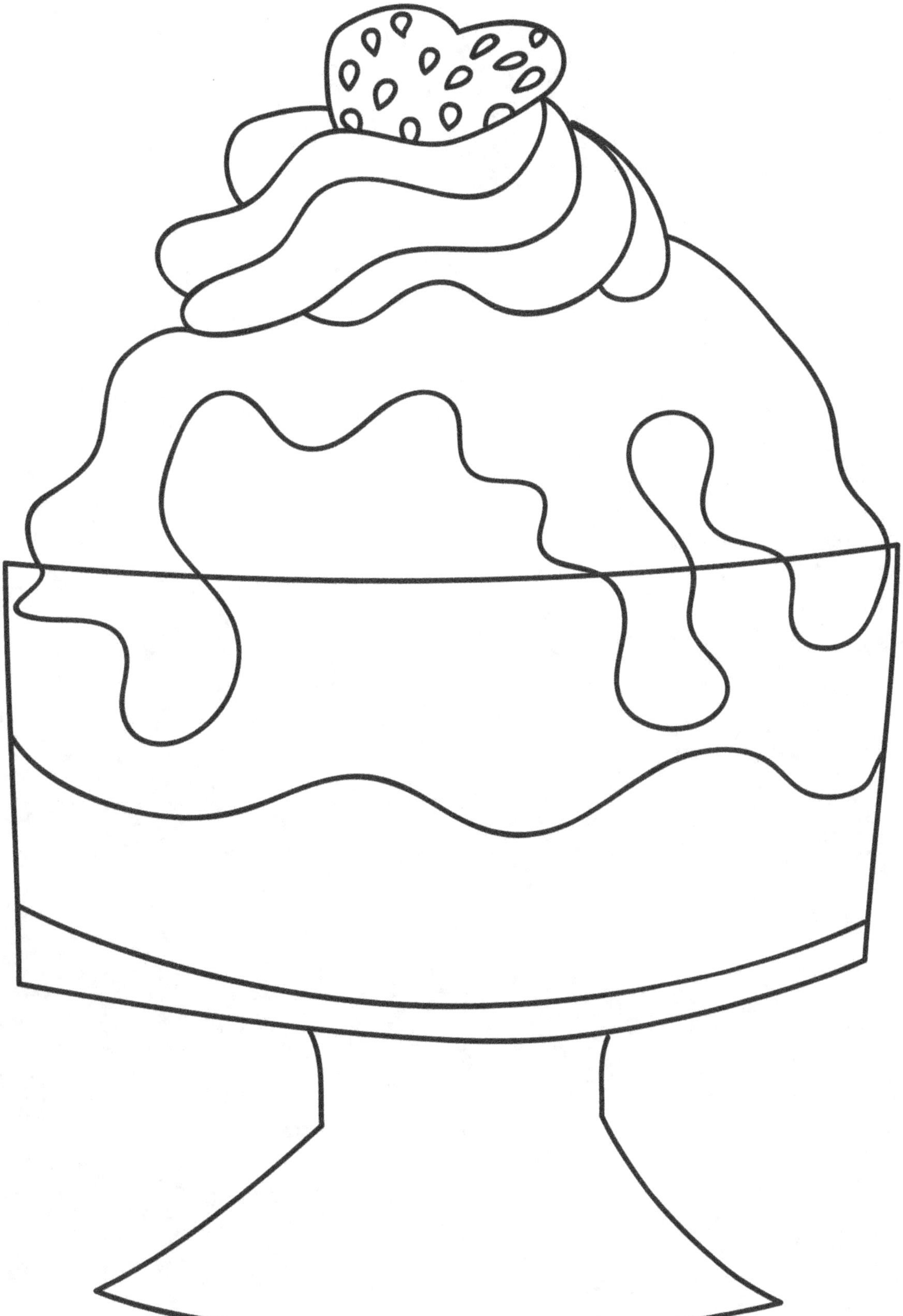

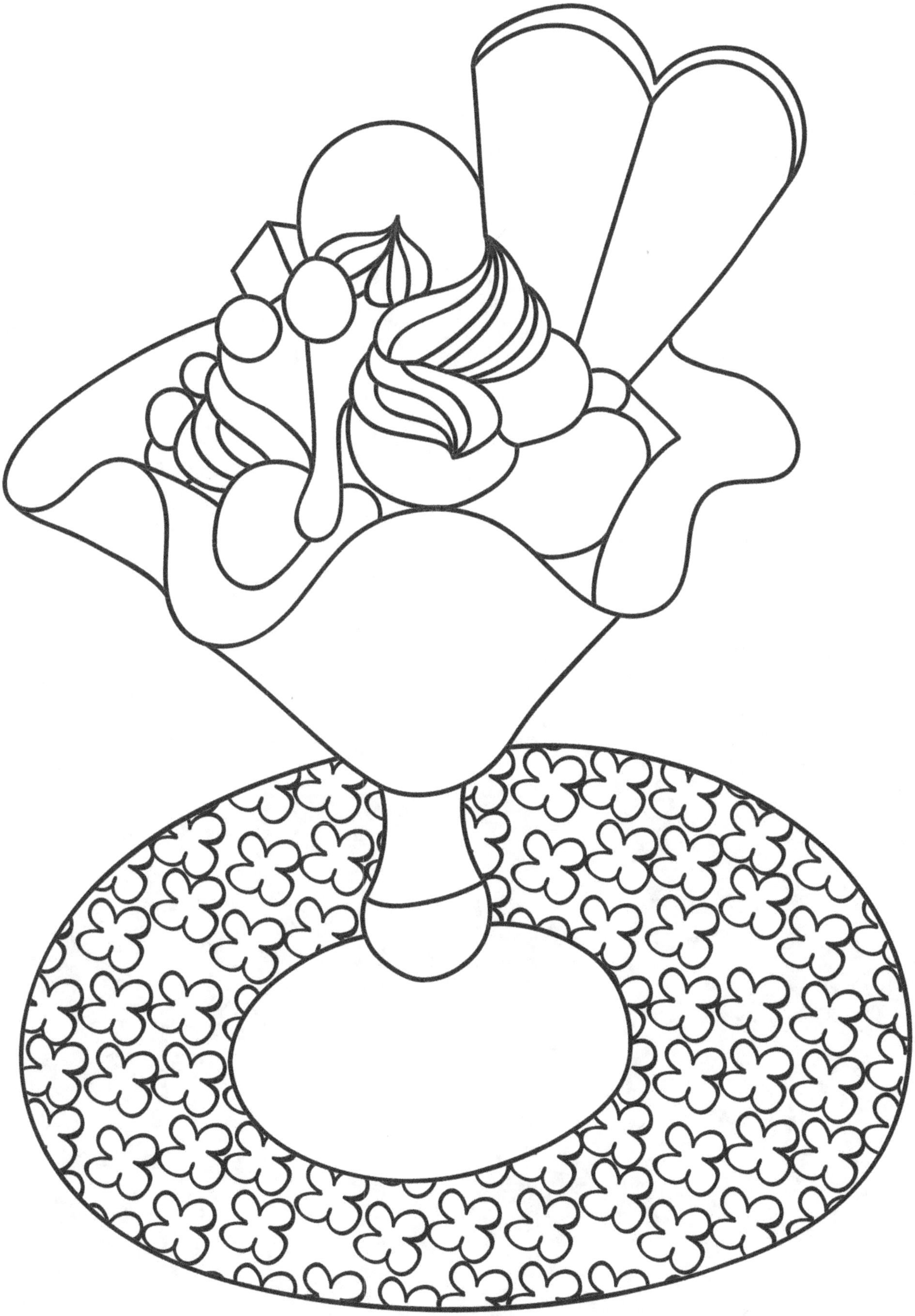

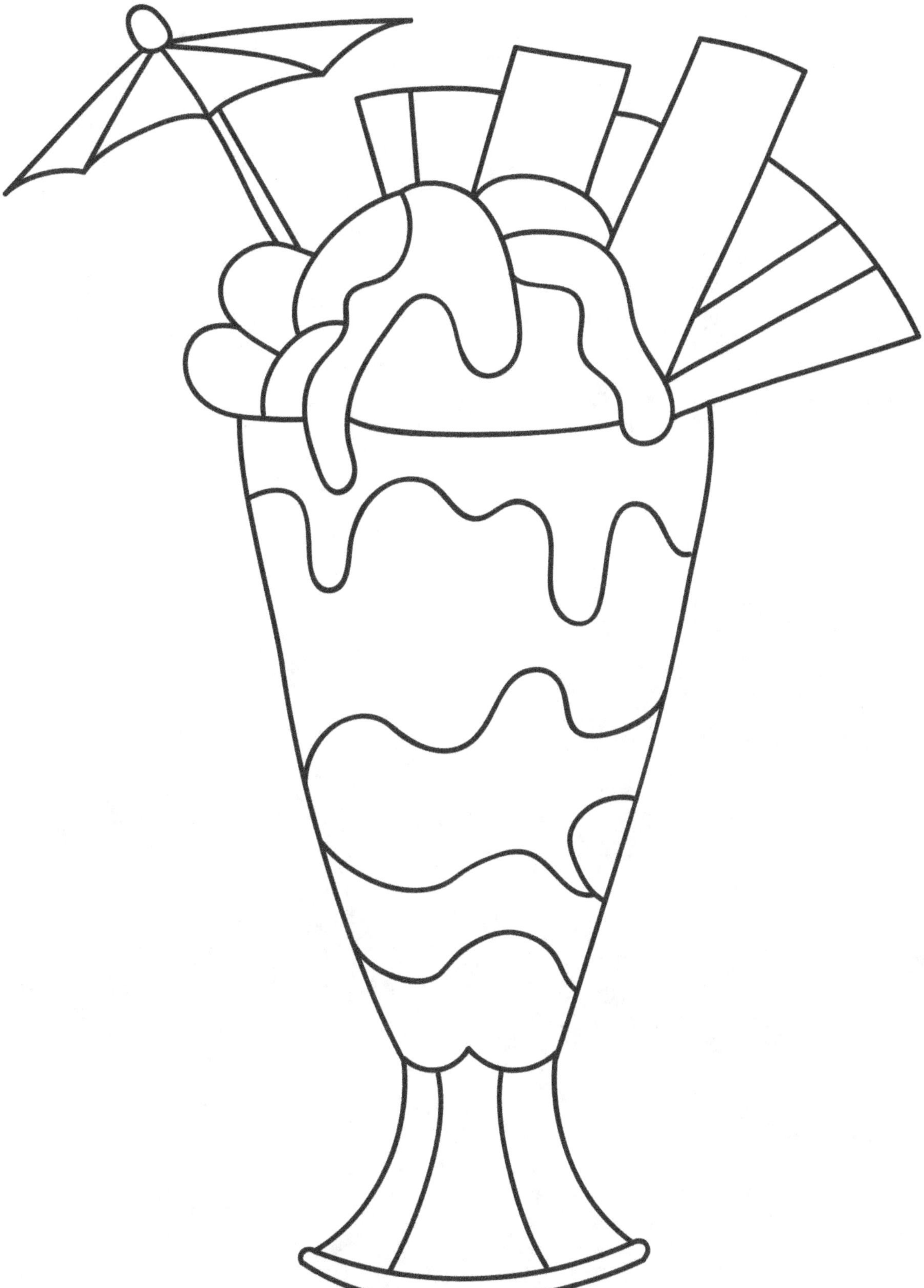

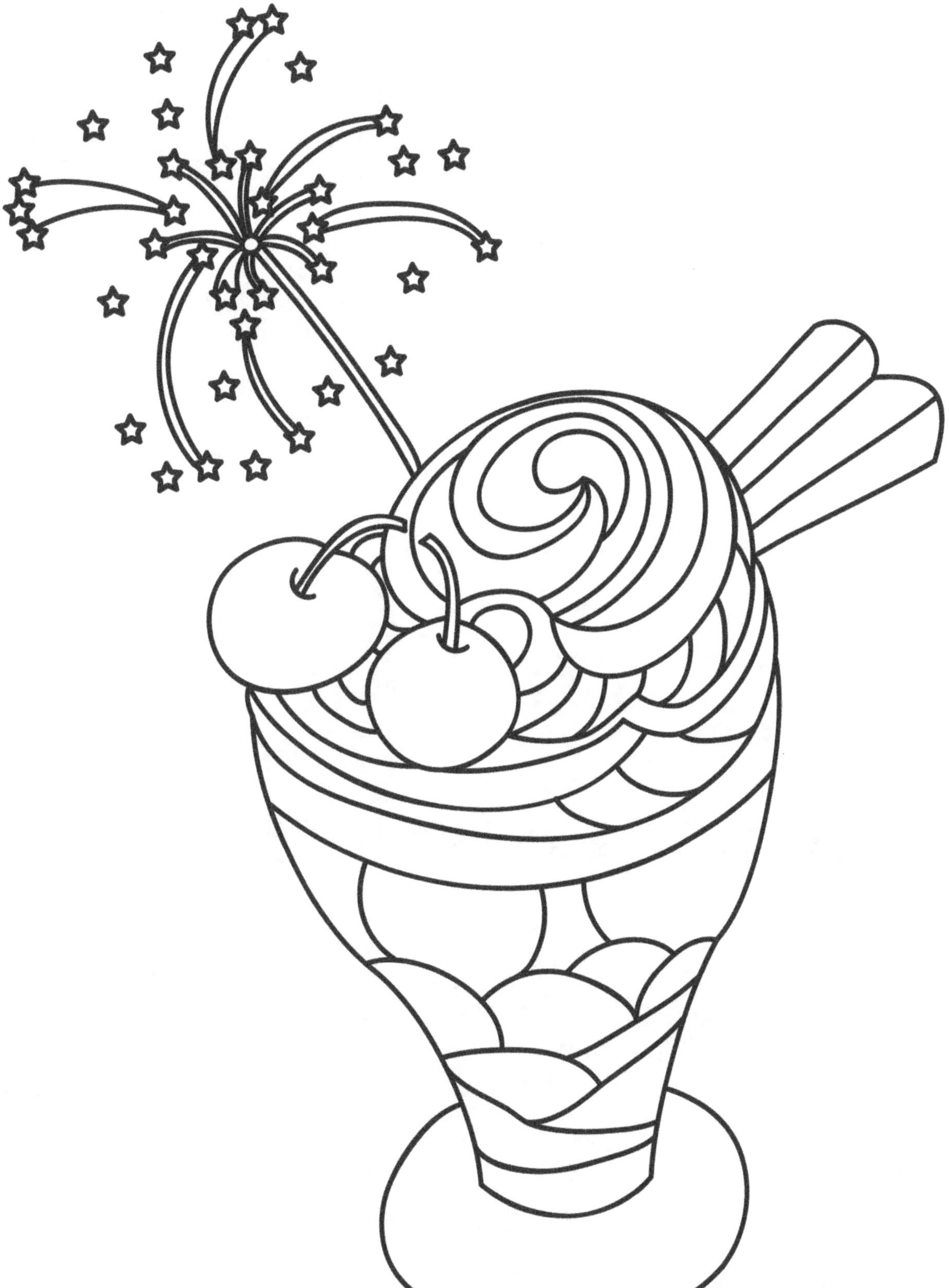

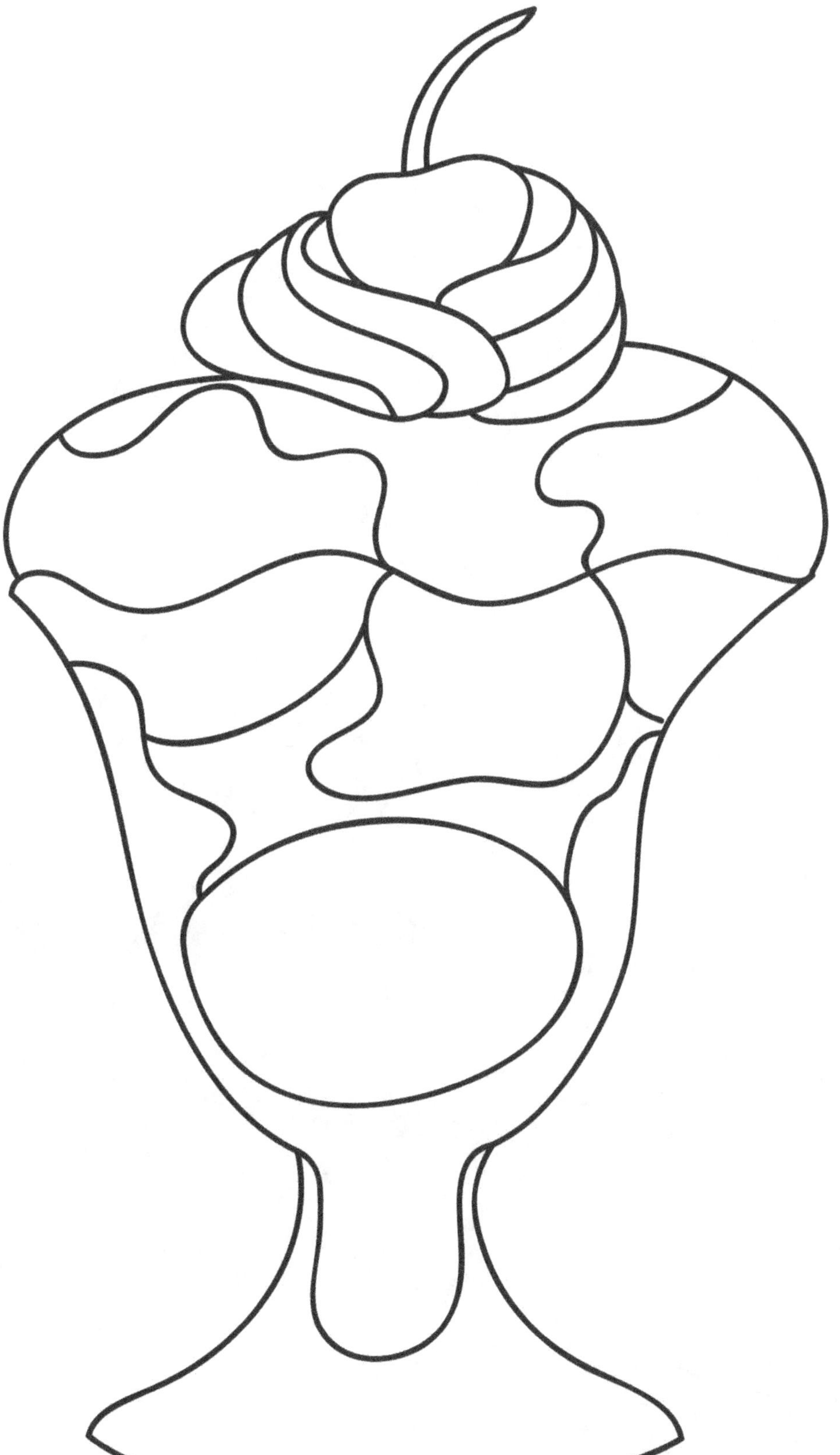

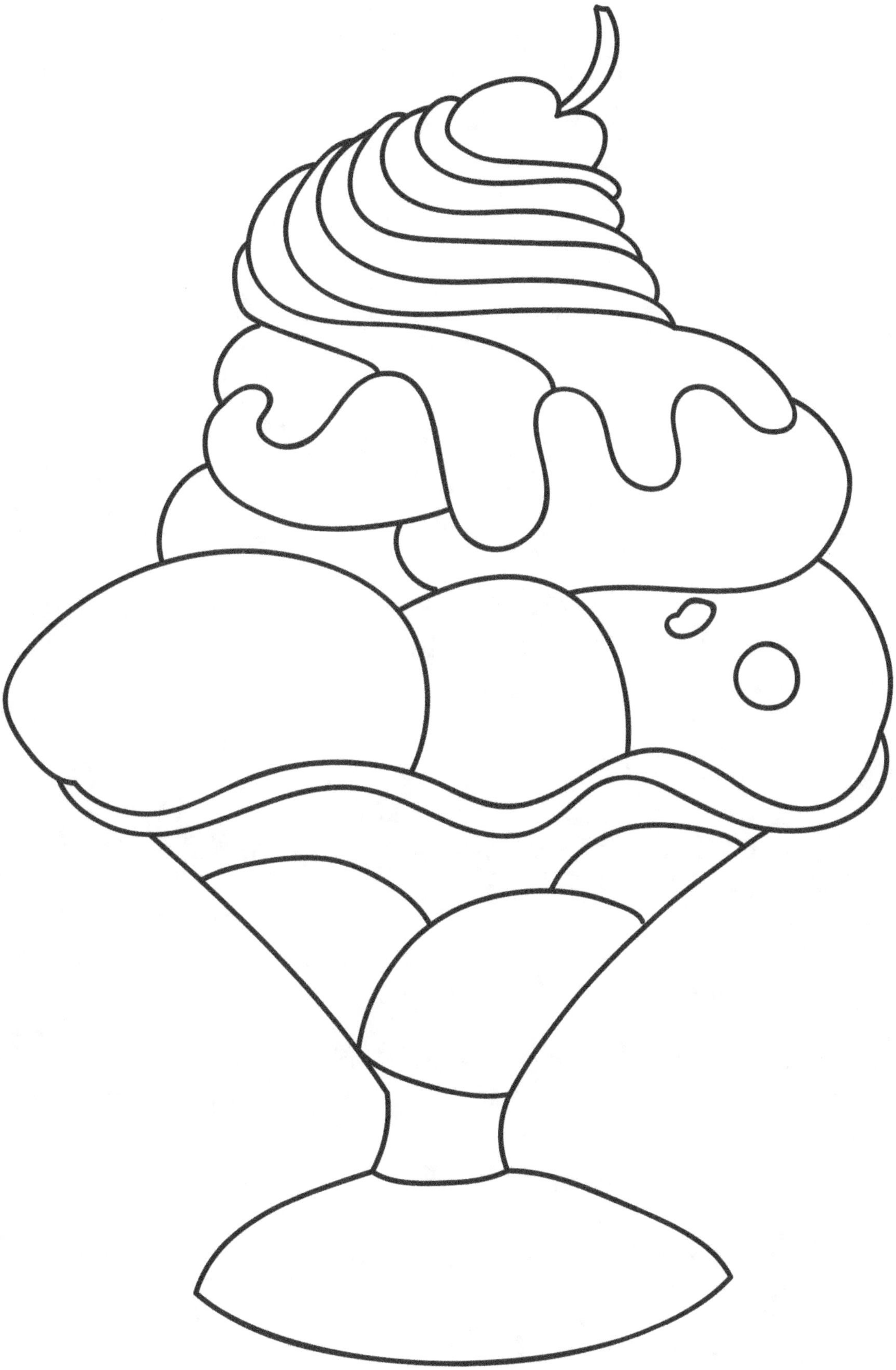

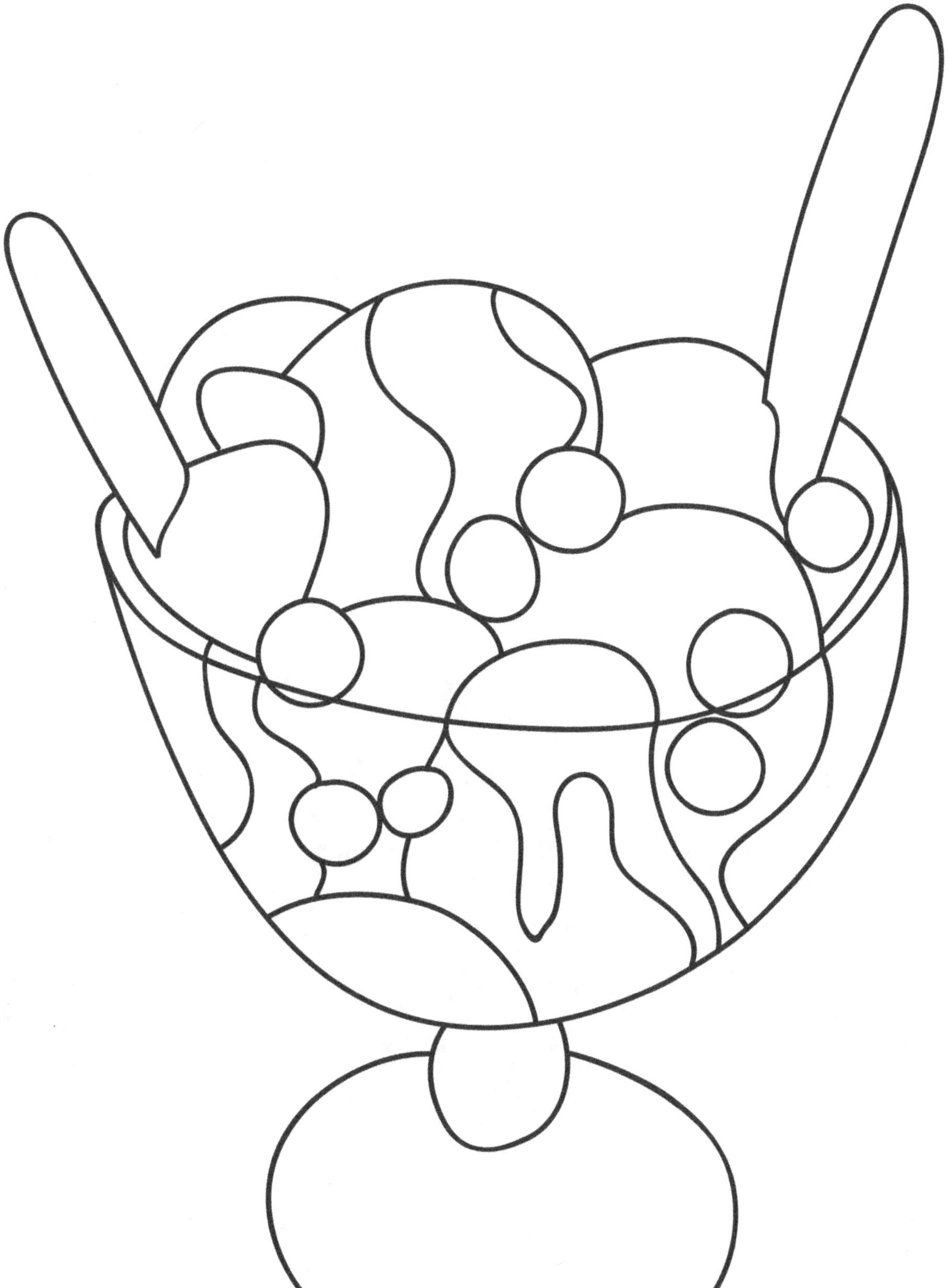

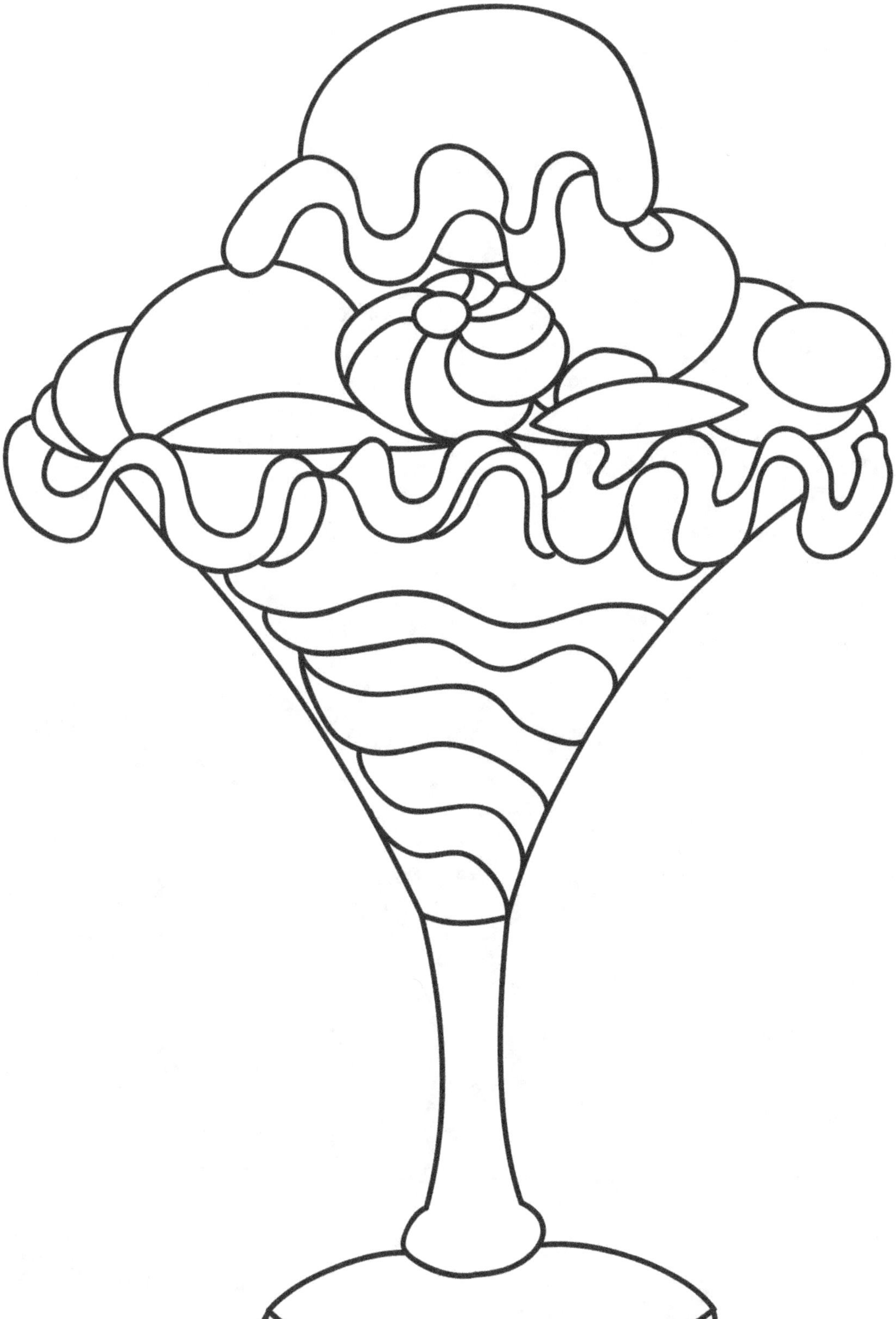

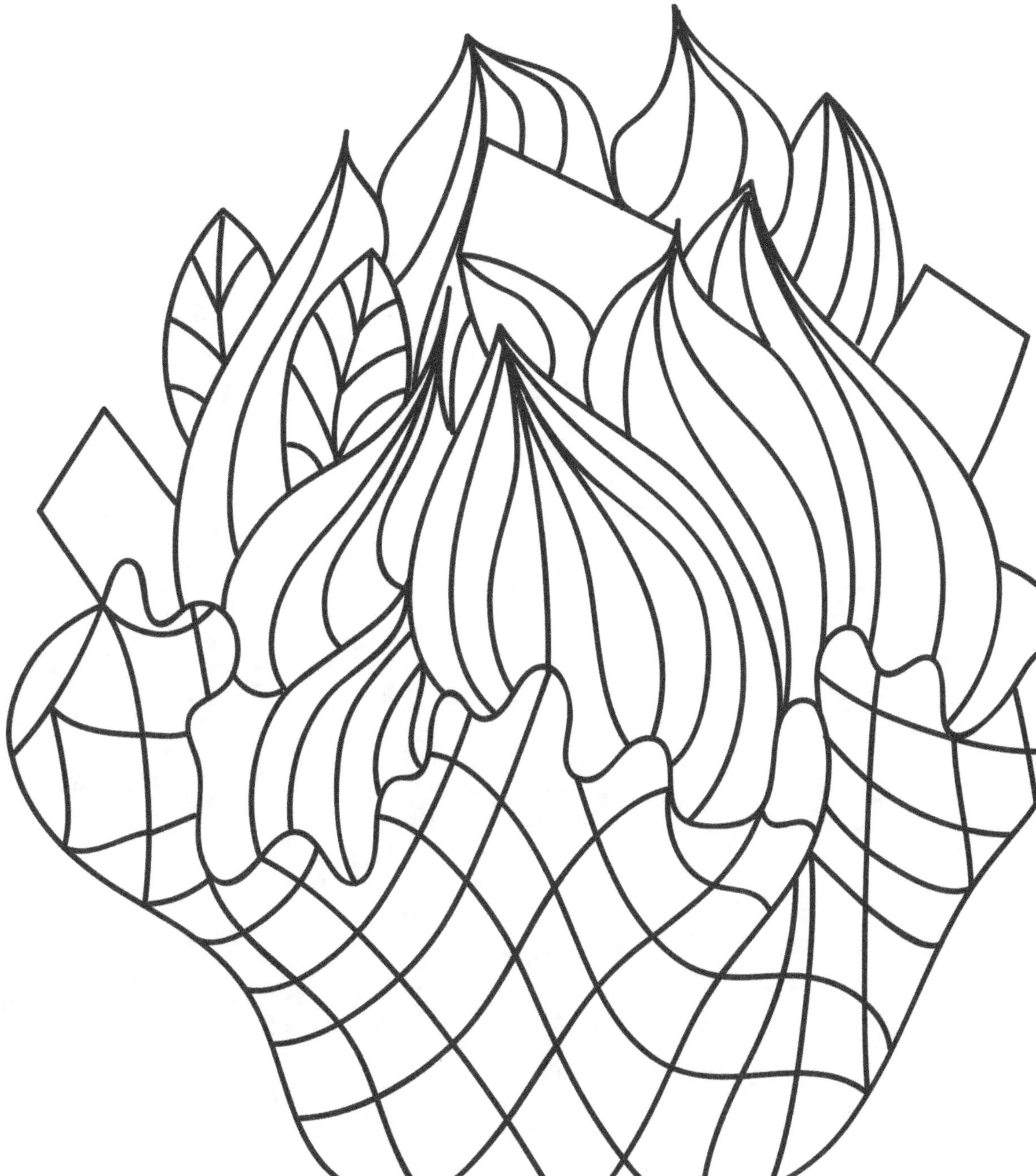

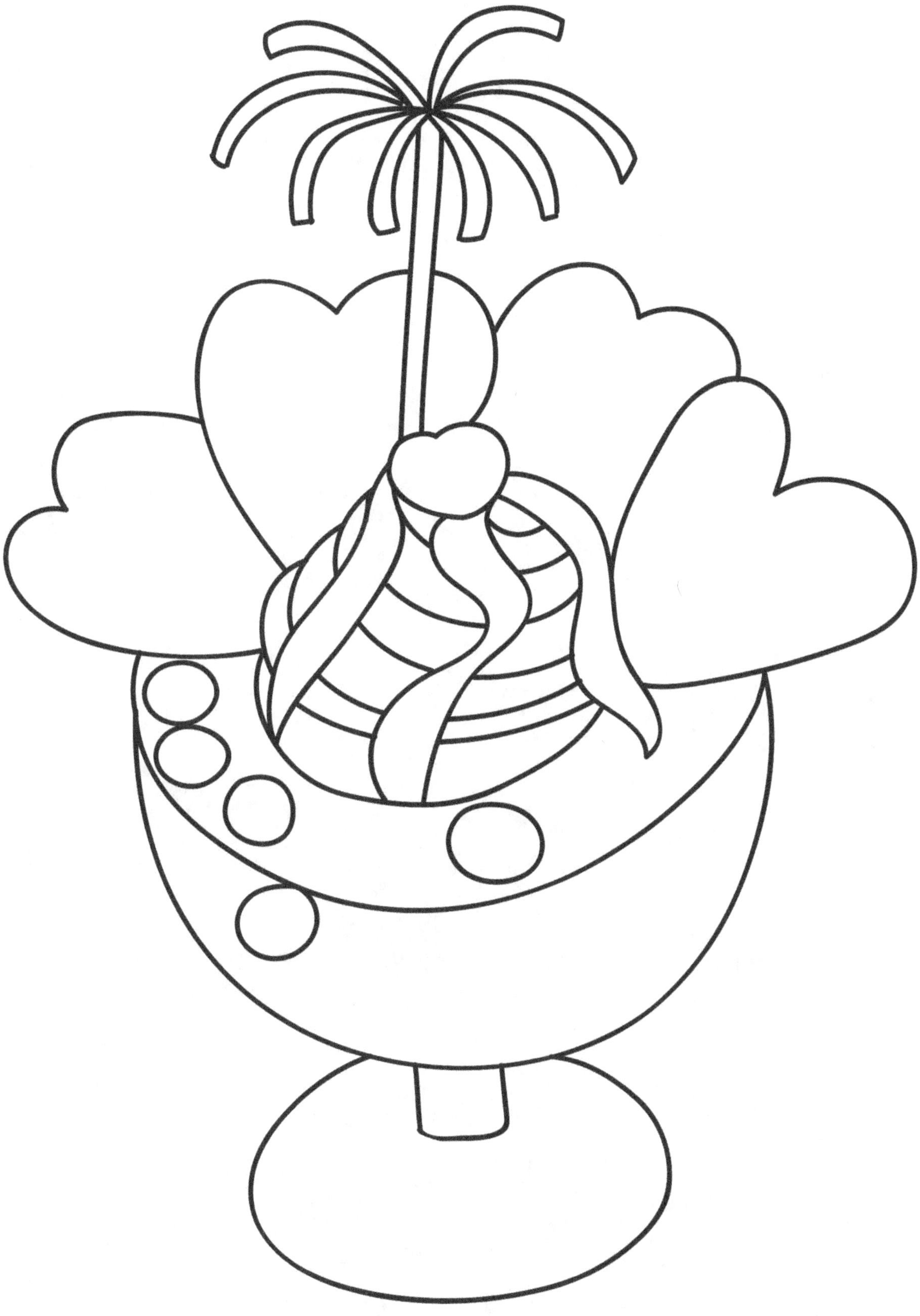

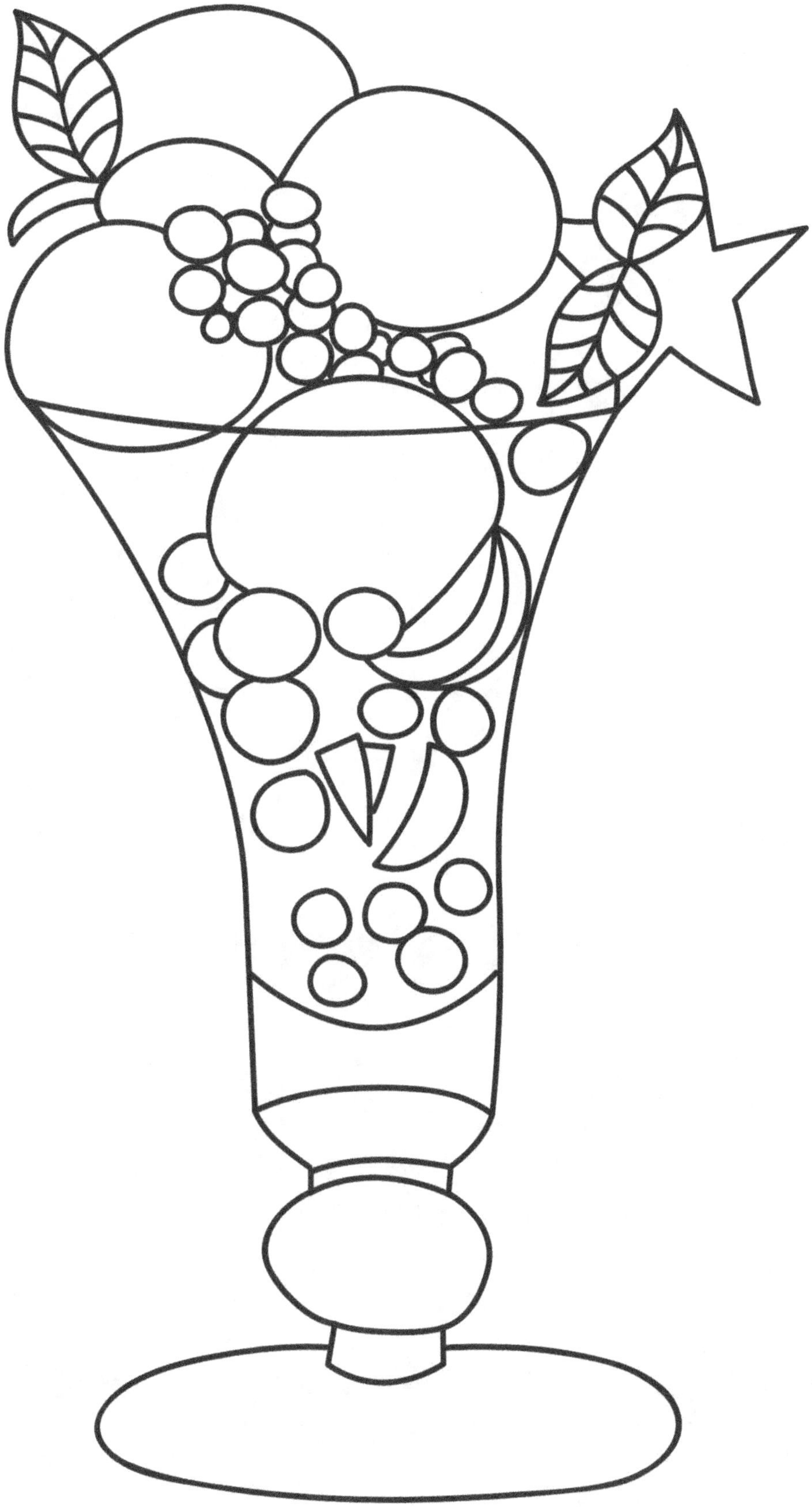

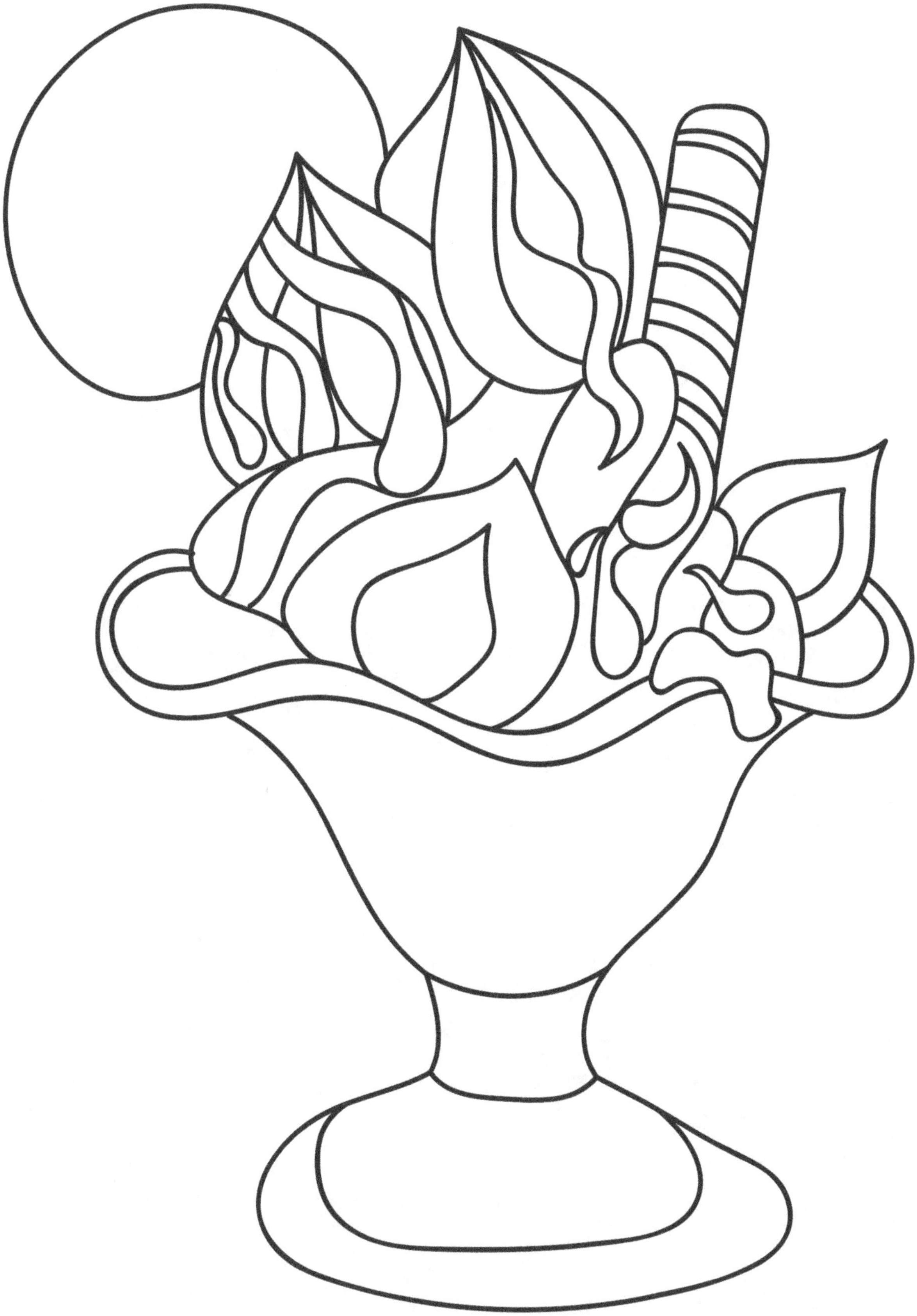

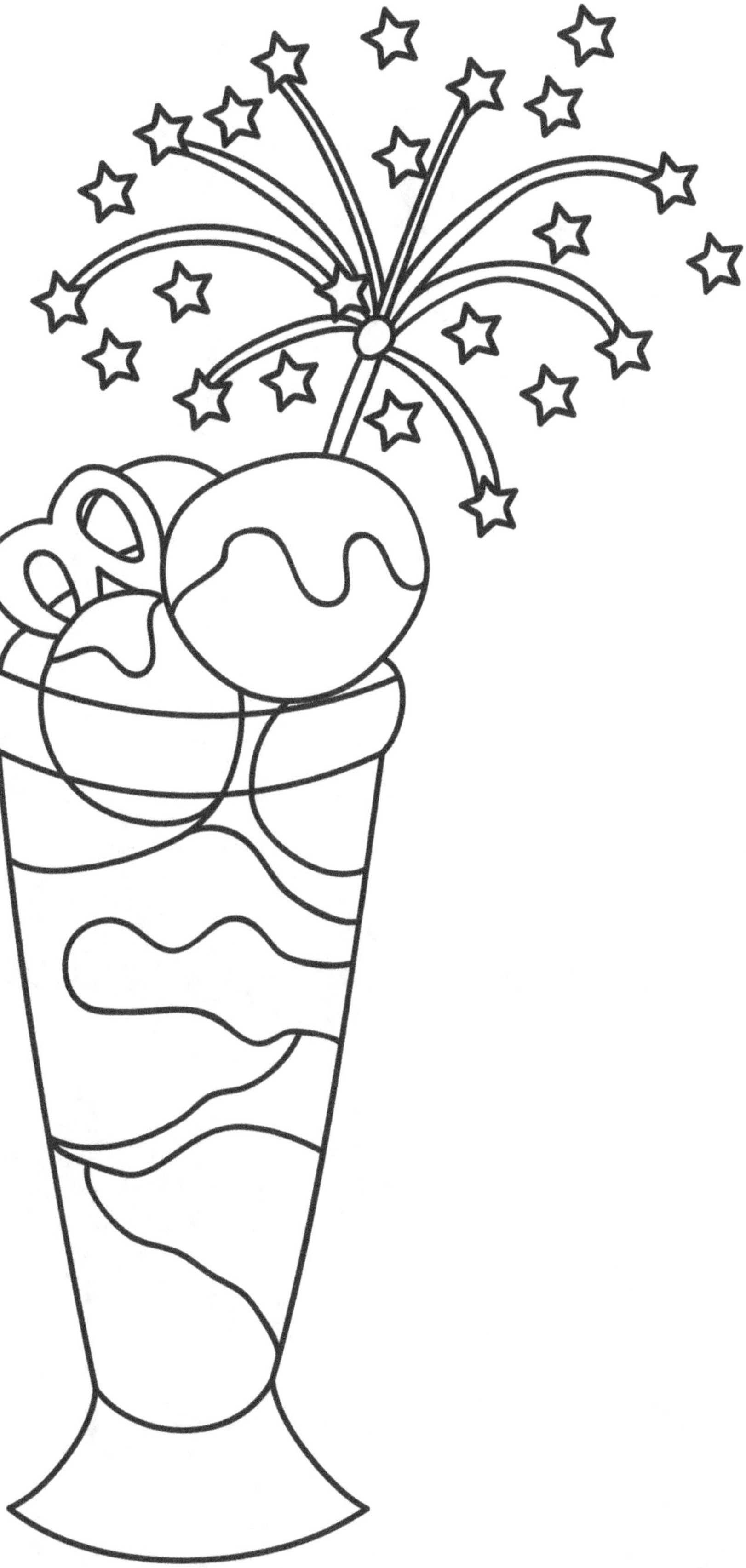

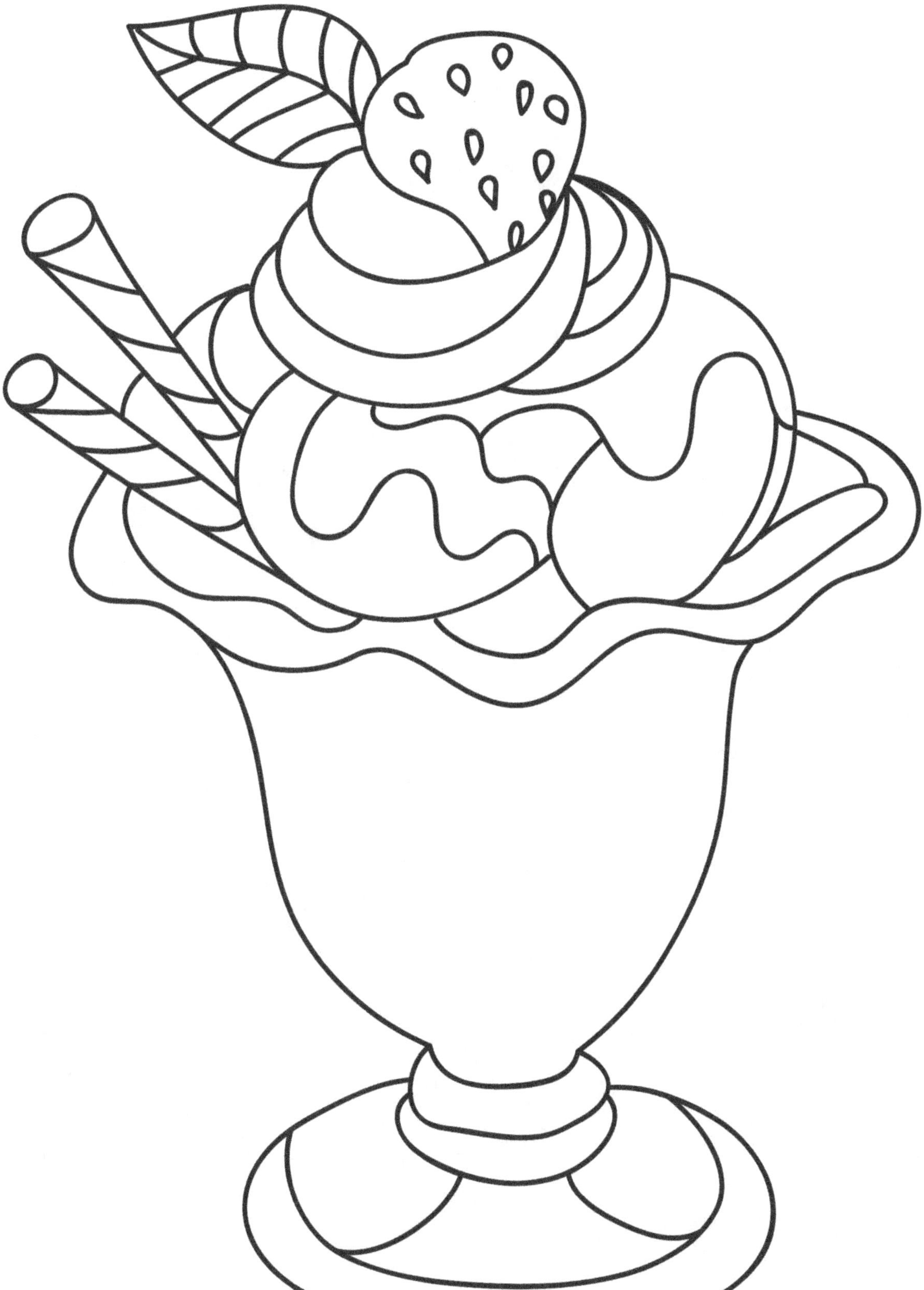

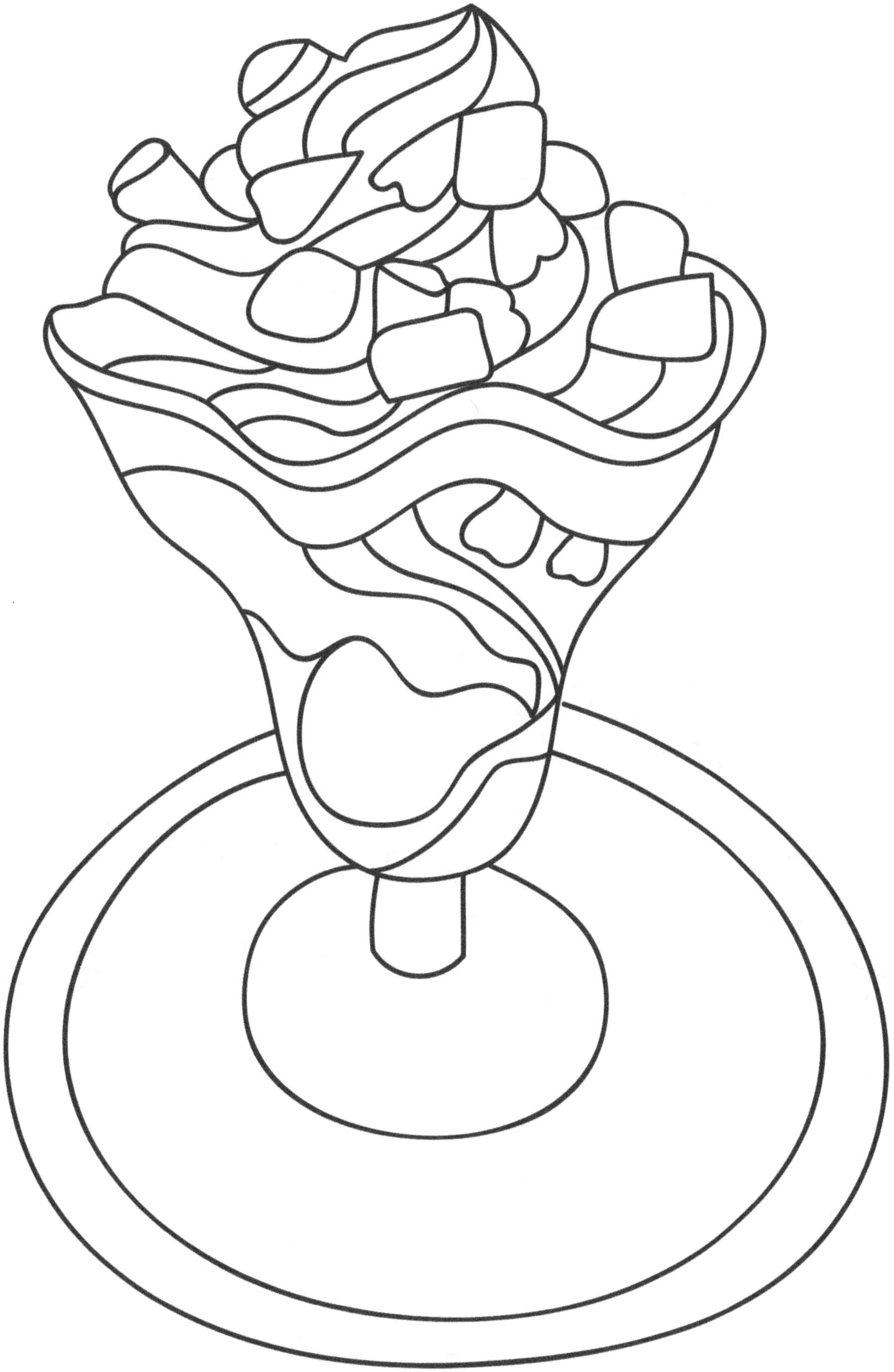

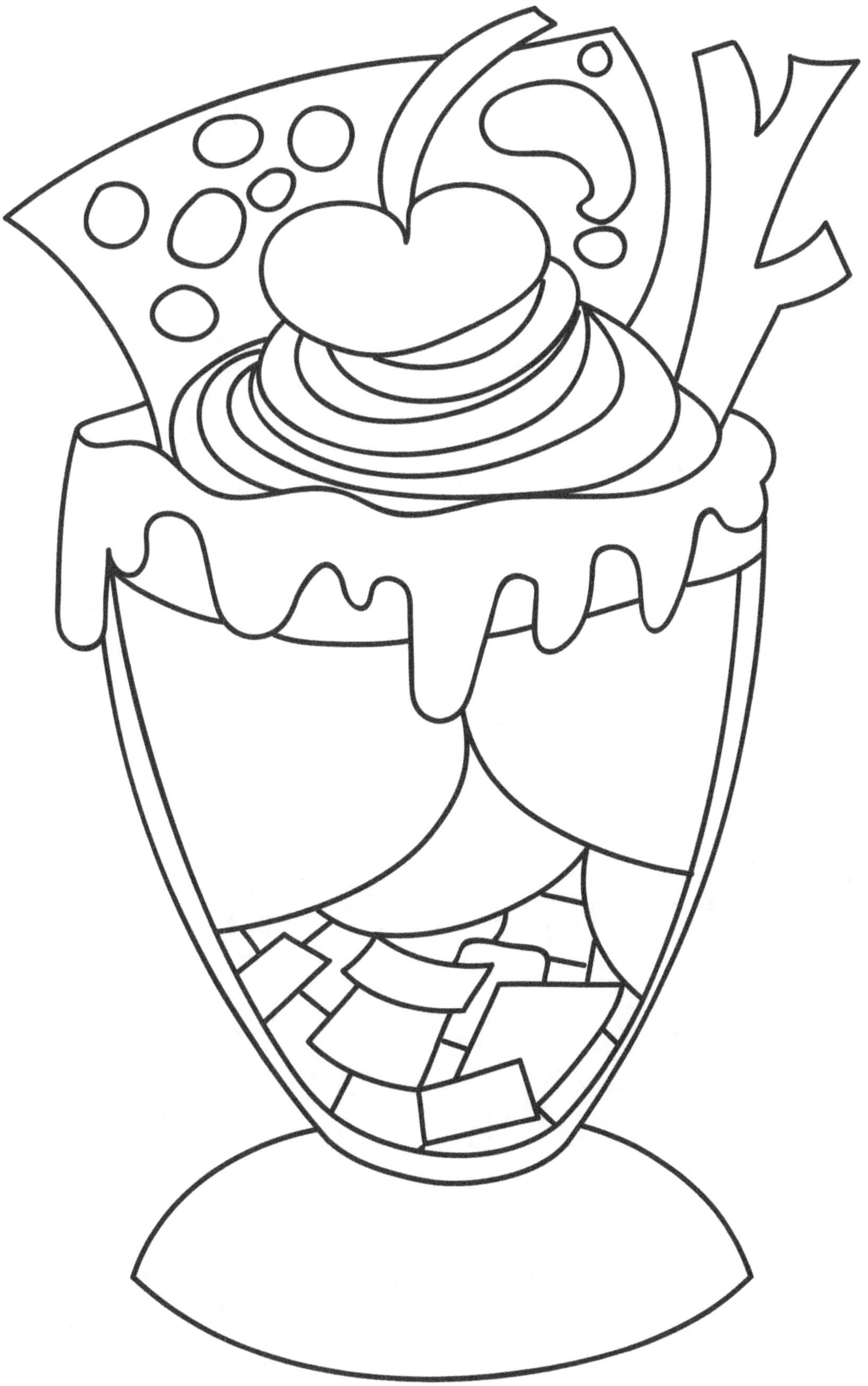

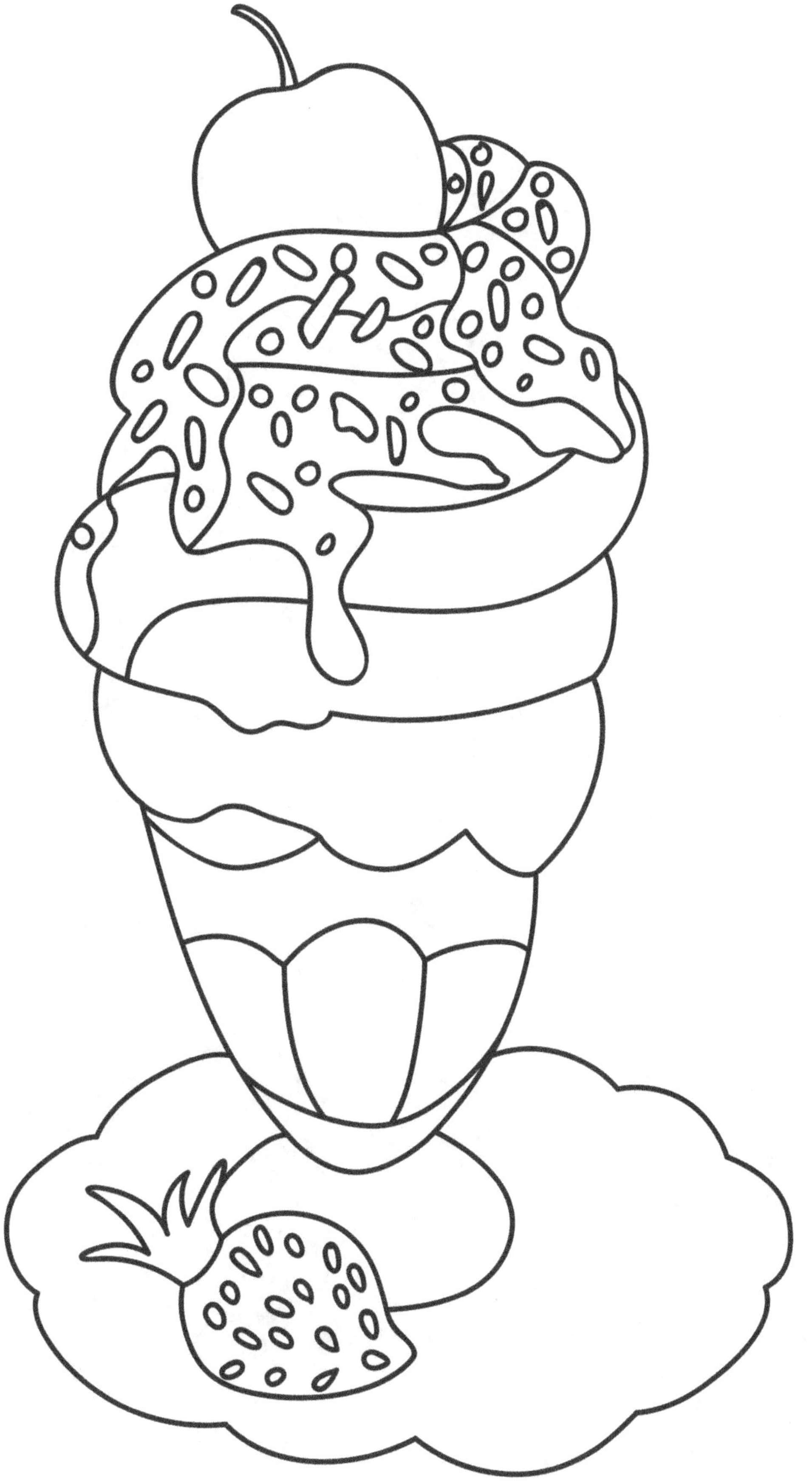

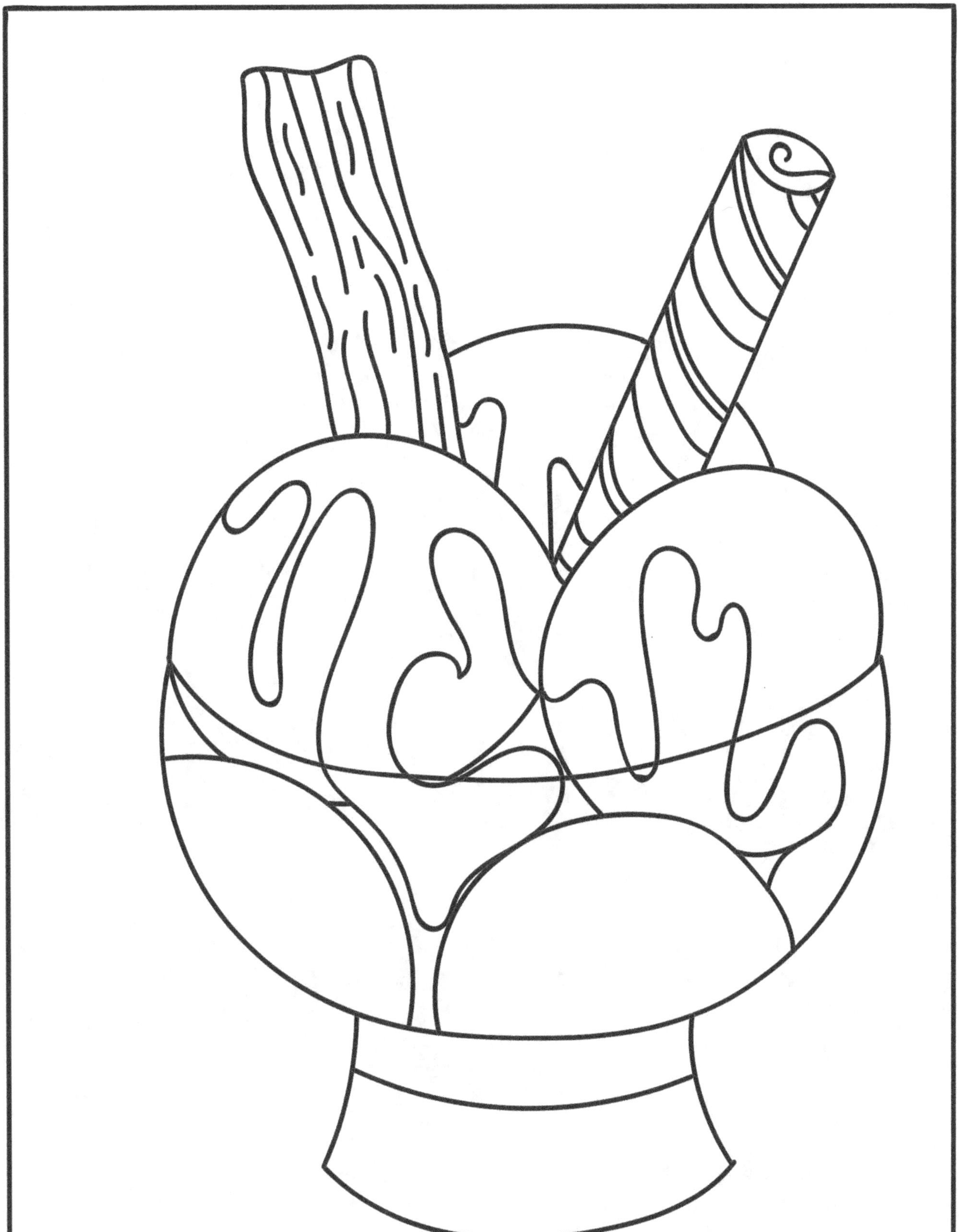

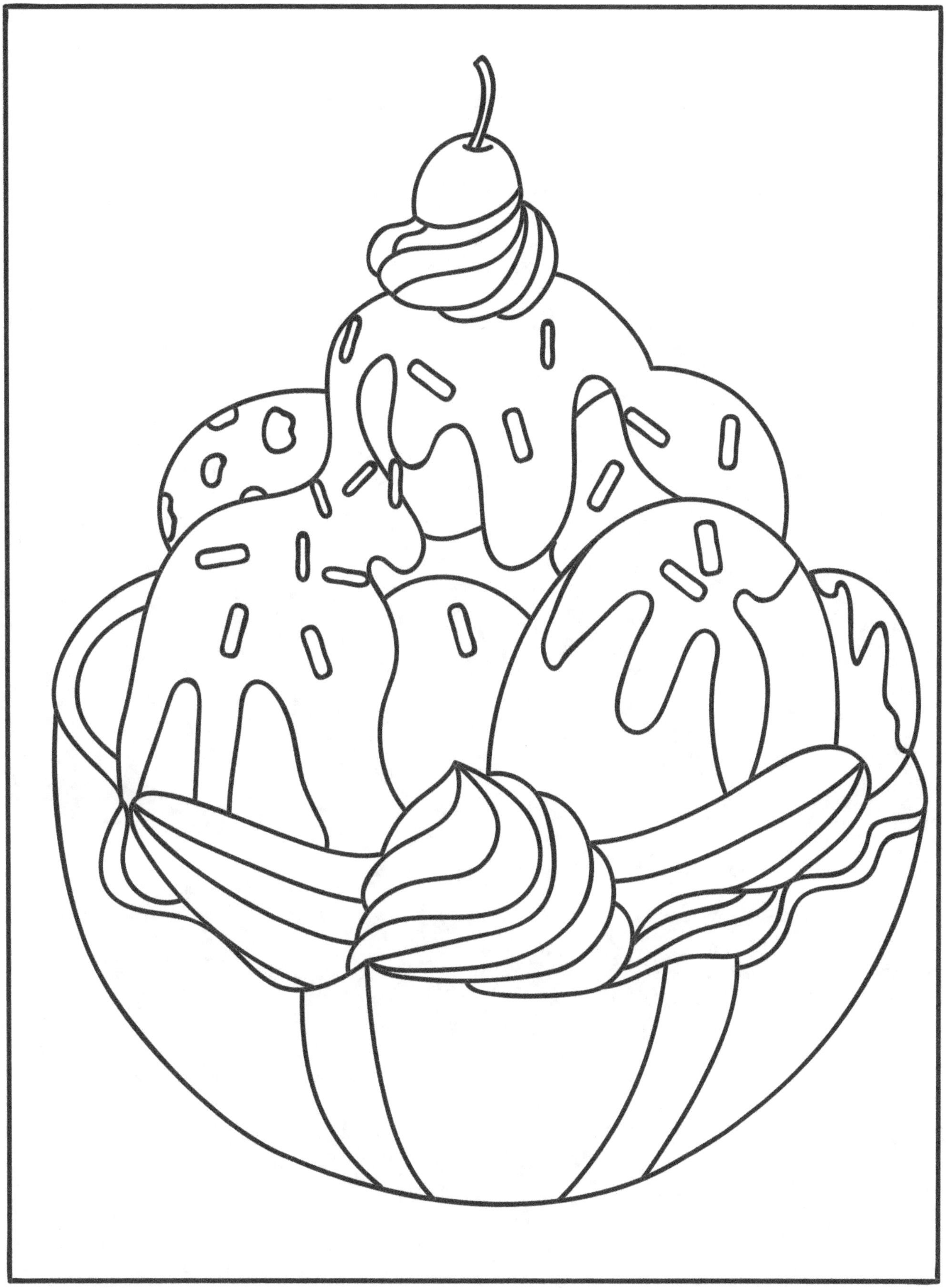

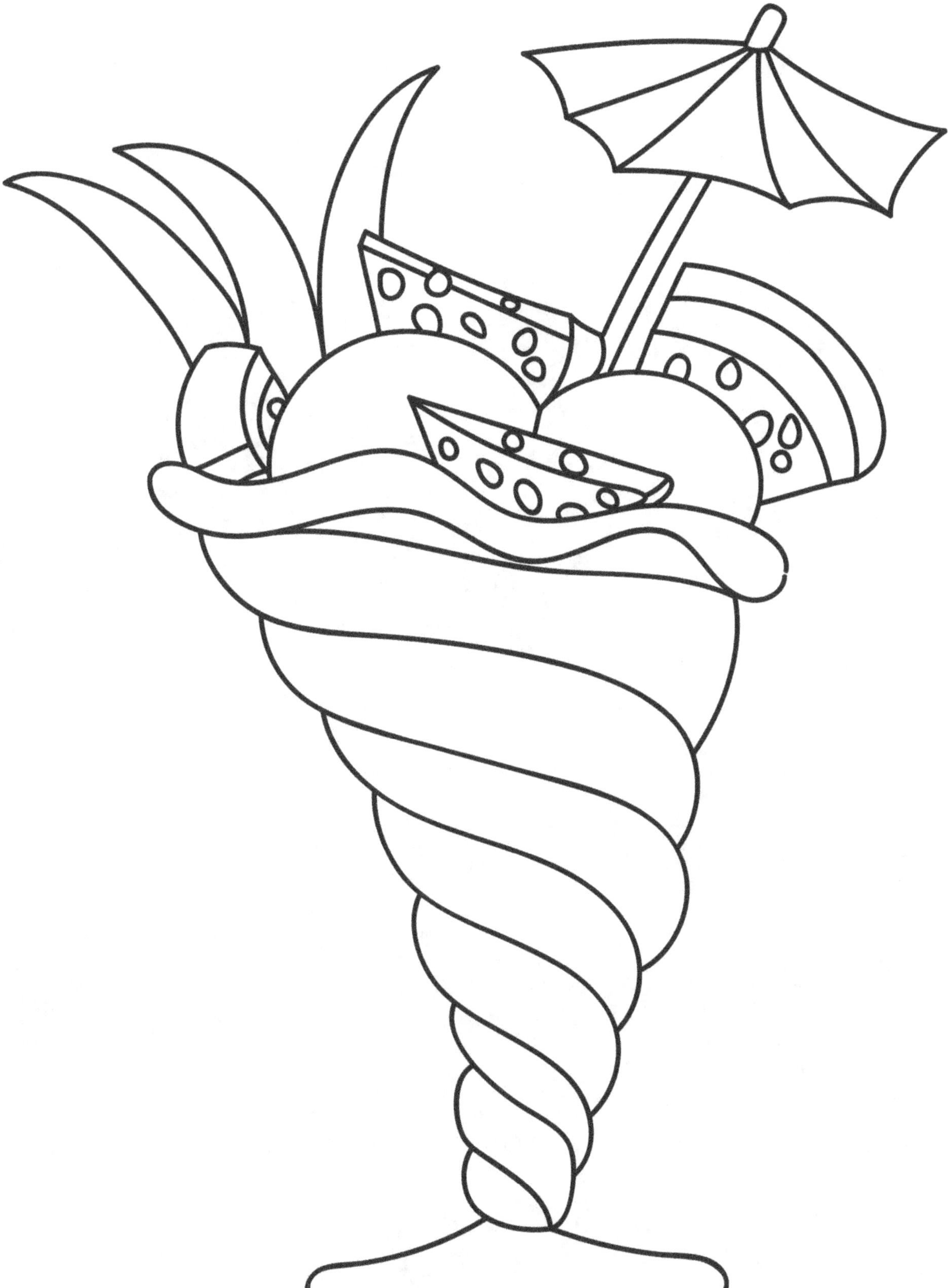

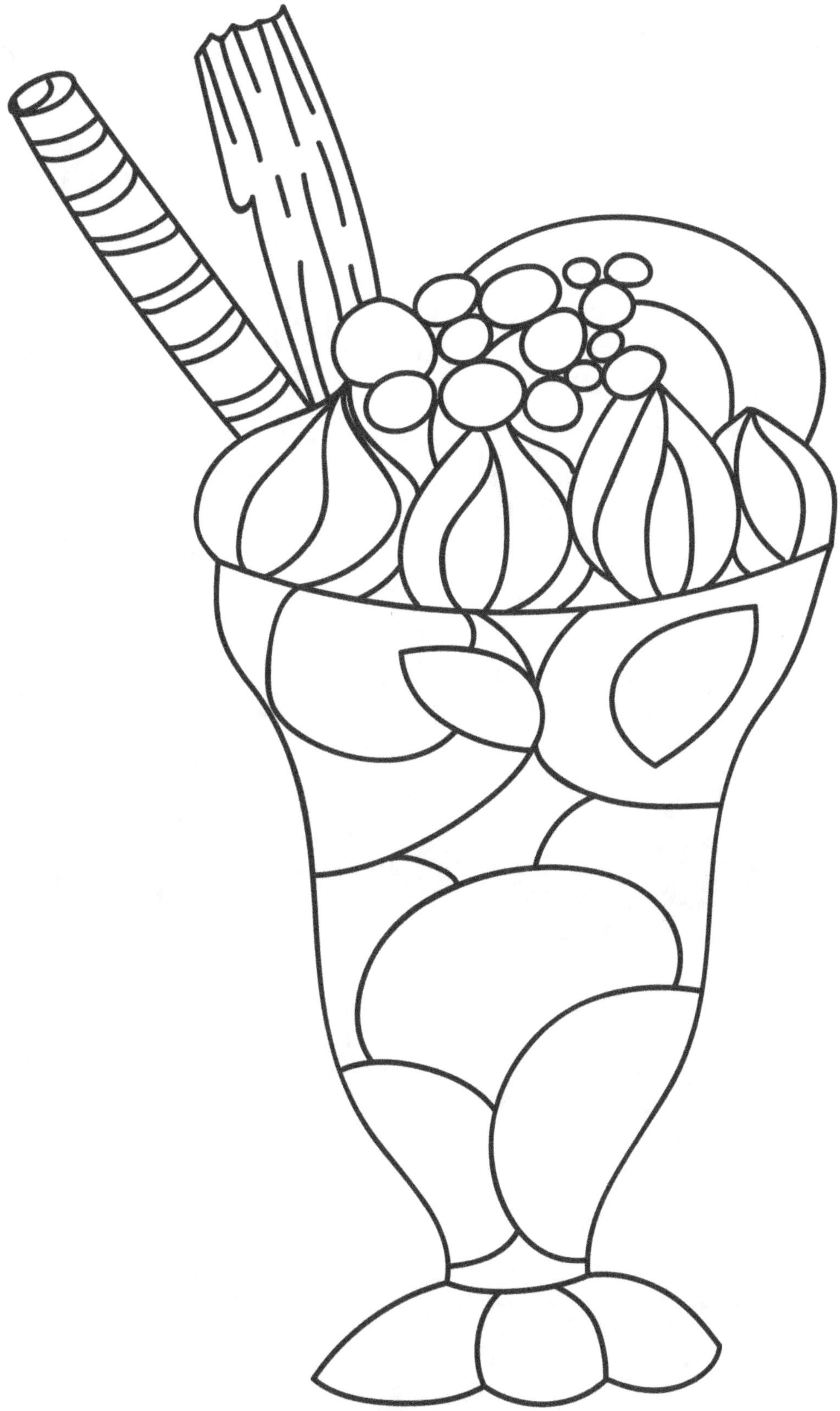

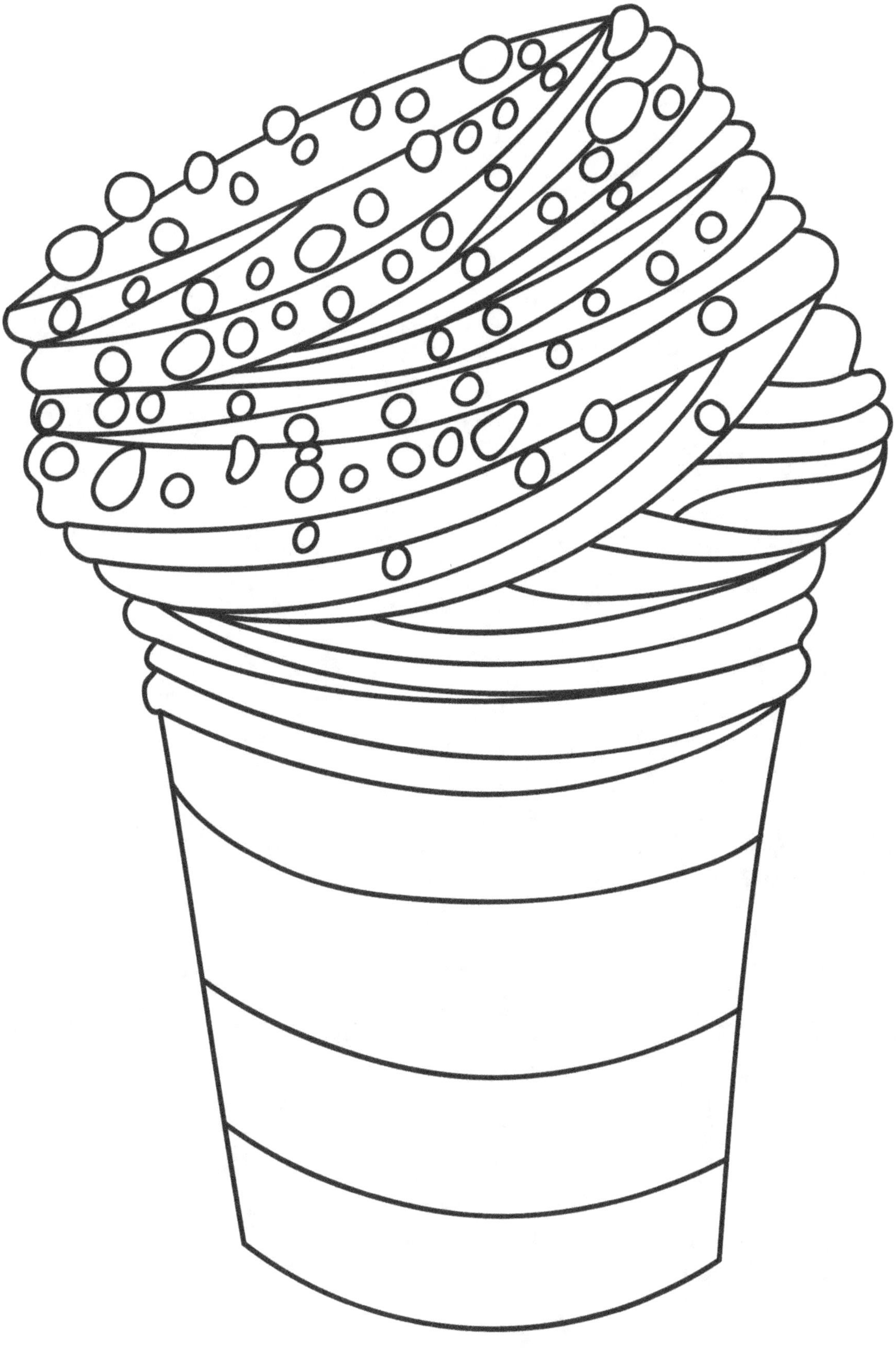

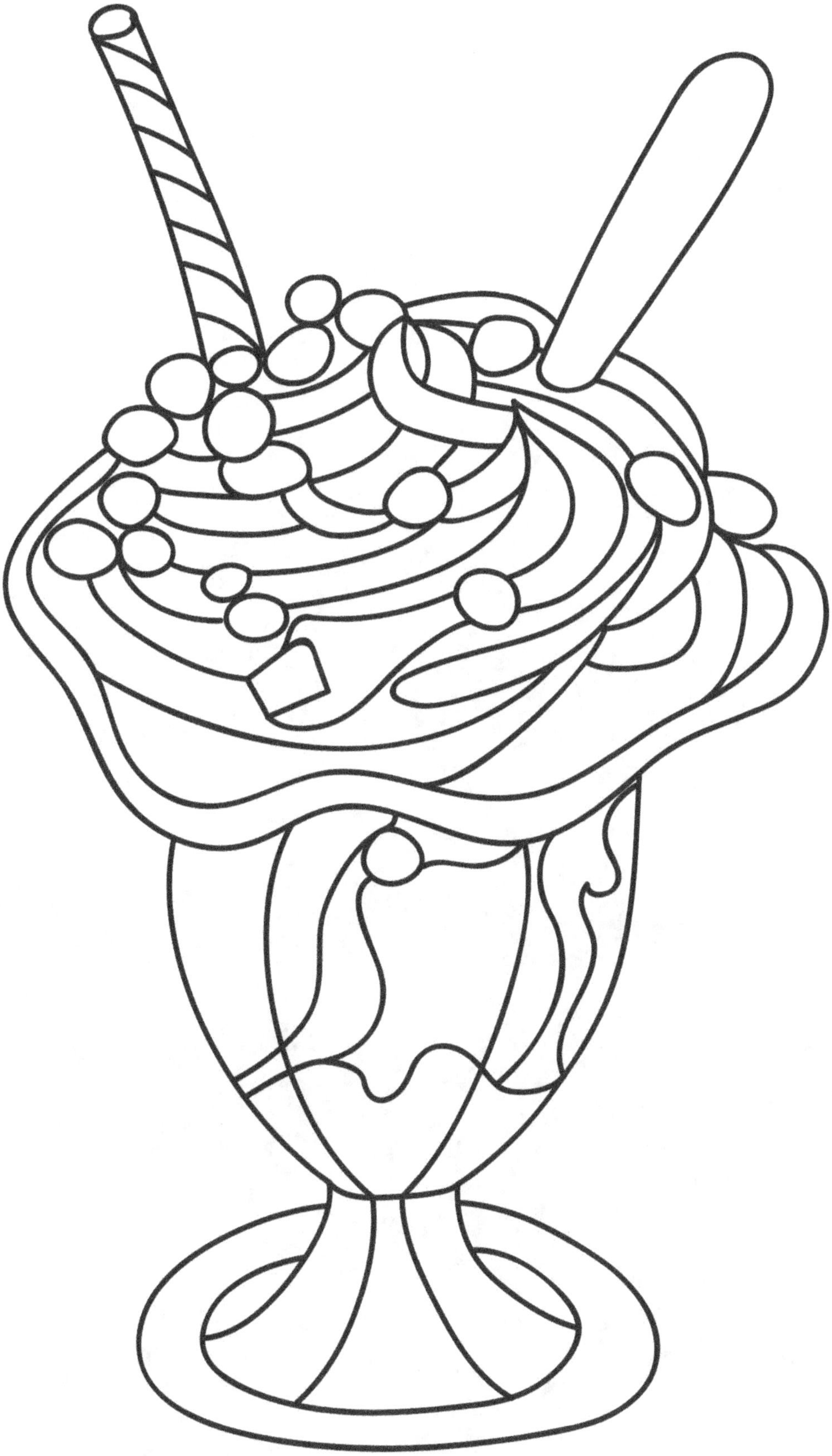

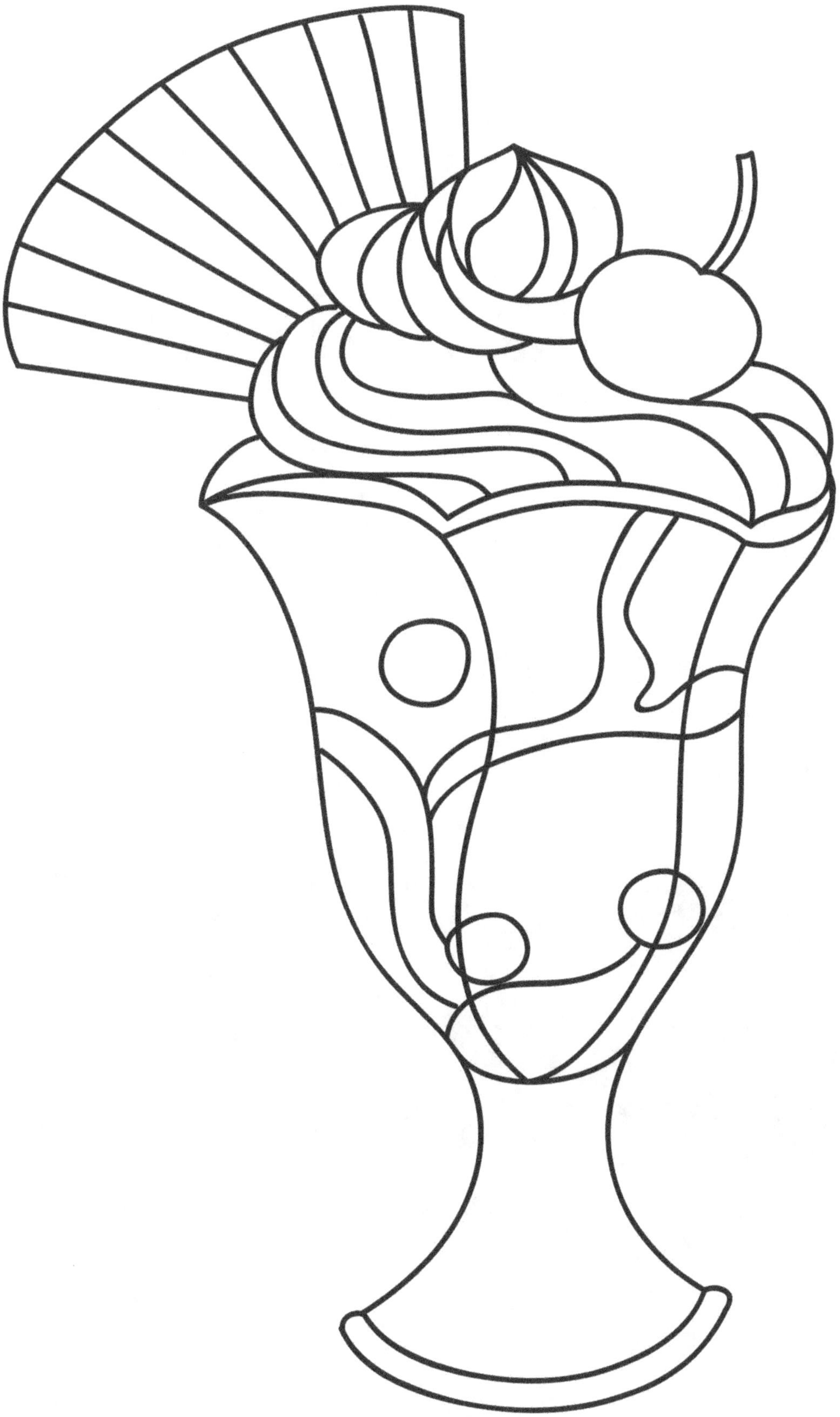

COLOR TEST PAGE

COLOR TEST PAGE

www.ingramcontent.com/pod-product-compliance
Lightning Source LLC
Chambersburg PA
CBHW081016170526
45158CB00010B/3056
9781090496201